Dedication

This book is dedicated to the many small businesses that operate because of the dedicated owners behind them. You continue to impress me every day with your ingenuity and passion. You are the driving force behind the innovation in our economy. It is your inspiration that pushes me forward.

Contents

Introduction

Nothing is more important than businesses to propel the economy forward. The United States is certainly a land of opportunity where, depending on the industry, you can start a business with a minimal amount of work. Most of the time it is spending a couple of hours online getting a Tax ID number, business licenses, and registering with the correct departments.

There is something about a free spirit who decides to go the non-traditional route and make their own mark in the world and start a business. There are businesses that will thrive and others that will fail miserably. But there are no guarantees in life, in fact the Declaration of Independence said we have the right to pursue happiness. We might pursue it our entire lives and never achieve it, but we can keep pursuing.

We hold these truths to be self-evident, that all men are created equal, that they are endowed by their Creator with certain unalienable Rights, that among these are Life, Liberty, and the pursuit of Happiness. -Declaration of Independence paragraph two

There are a lot of business owners who pursue their happiness by making a mark in the world. They may get tired of working for someone else, making them money while they are paid a small portion. They may have found a passion that wasn't captured by someone else. Ultimately, they may have an idea that hasn't been discovered or commercialized.

Remember when I said that starting a business is minimal work? Yeah, well that is the registration. The real work comes in form of the blood, sweat, and tears that you will put into your labor of love. Just like our own children, our business becomes an extension of ourselves and we will do anything to make it succeed.

Not everyone understands the long days, the stressing over money, the countless rejections, and even the self-doubt that may creep as you start to question your sanity. But then there is that point, the point where you sit back and realize this is going to work, you are going to be successful. Congratulations, you have made it!

It is at that point you need to start rewarding yourself for the work that you have accomplished. You might have put everything you have ever saved into your business. While you will want to continue to invest in your business, you also need to diversify away from it. The business is currently successful but we don't know what tomorrow will hold.

Now you get the opportunity to reward yourself and your employees with a retirement plan. Maybe you have done a little research online or you talked to your buddy at the bar or on the golf course. He has told you emphatically that this is the only plan you should go with. You will talk to a couple of different providers and they will give you a bunch of options and tell you to choose one. Oh, and by the way, each option comes with many other choices.

If there was only a way to simplify this process? Now there is, this book was designed to simplify the process of choosing a retirement plan that is suitable for where you are currently. As you grow as a business owner and as a company you will find that the plan you chose is no longer suitable. Please keep this book around because what you will find is that you might switch retirement plans several times during your tenure as an owner. Please, try to find a trusted advisor who works independently so they can give you an honest answer about the pros and cons of the plans you are considering.

Your work is going to fill a large part of your life, and the only way to be truly satisfied is to do what you believe is great work. And the only way to do great work is to love what you do-Steve Jobs, Co-founder of Apple Inc.

Small Business is a Big Deal

This book isn't being marketed to the CEO of Apple or Microsoft, even though I'd be flattered if they read it. This book is geared toward the small business owner. You might aspire to be a large company one day, or just maintain an employee head count of one. Where ever you want to go, you are not alone in your quest. According to the Small Business & Entrepreneurship Council there were 5.73 million employer firms in the US in 2012. Of those, 99.7% had less than 500 employees and 89.6% had less than 20 employees. In addition to being the innovators in the economy, small businesses have added 60% of all new jobs since 2009.

Small business truly is the innovator when it comes to the economy. Small businesses that produce patents have 16 times more patents per employee than large patenting firms. Often the energy, focus, and flexibility of a small firm allows it to be more innovative in what they do. Many of the most innovative small firms get purchased or merge with larger firms. If it wasn't for their innovations many of the technological advances we have today wouldn't exist if someone hadn't pushed the envelope on what was possible.

Being closer to clients, understanding the market, and being able to adapt quickly often provides small firms the capability work in niches that large companies fail to see, or don't see profitable enough to pursue. Small business provides a quality service to those who don't fit in the boxes that large corporations design. And it shows, smalls firms produce nearly 50% of the GDP in the United States and have a large import/export presence.

Small business is a big deal and for that reason you need to think big about yourself and your business. My goal is to provide a quality service to the small business owner, debunking some myths about retirement plans, and providing a clear path to choosing a retirement plan that is appropriate for you.

This book isn't designed to be all encompassing when it comes to retirement plans. In fact, this book is designed to help you pinpoint the one or two plans that will satisfy most of your needs. At that point, you can work with a company or trusted advisor to work out the details and address additional questions. It is there job to affirm the plan will meet your needs. There are books that cover each plan, this is way too much information and it doesn't help you to reach your goal as a business owner. After all you specialize in what you do and that is where your focus should be.

Myths Debunked

I'm going to address some of the myths I often hear about when business owners talk about retirement plans.

- <u>Retirement plans are too expensive</u>
  - o Depending on the retirement plan there could be additional cost involved. However, if you are looking at one of the start-up plans there is rarely a cost above the commission paid (some offer no-load funds). The more complex the plan the more it will cost, if you are viewing those options you would be more concerned about how much you can put away than the cost to set-up the retirement account.
- <u>I'll just sell my company to fund retirement</u>
  - o This can happen, but rarely does it work as planned. Many businesses, unless they have a unique niche, aren't worth as much as you imagine. If your company is a service provider for small stores and has a profitable route established, you might find it is the relationships that bring in the business. Any competitor could take over that territory without having to buy it from you. Once you are out of the picture the company could be worthless. If you established a strong brand and large client list, it could be worth something, but your dreams of retiring on a beach could be dashed.
  - o This isn't to say your company doesn't have value, just be strategic in how and when you sell your business. Competitors know when you are selling to get out of the business or retire. You will get much more if they are taking over a territory and you are in position of naming a price.
- <u>My employees won't contribute</u>

- o I hear this all the time! From professional offices to cleaning services the owner is always concerned that they will go through the process of opening a retirement account and they will be the only ones that contribute. Then we will go through the process and 80-90% of their employees will sign-up and they are stunned. Your employees want to have control of their retirement and they know that a retirement plan is their best opportunity. An amazing thing happens after the enrollment, the employer finds that employees are now more engaged and more likely to stay with the company longer. This provides an additional sticking point for the employee.
- **I can't afford a match**
  - o There are multiple ways that you can match your employee's retirement plan. Much of this is dictated on the business owner and how much they are looking to contribute. You might not be able to match much initially, as little as 1%. Why bother? A Forbes articles, *Happy Employees=Hefty Profits,* found that happy employees led to higher profits, as much as 22% higher. Part of the reason was the benefits; a retirement plan is the second most sought after benefit behind health insurance. Provide a reason to attract great talent, keep your current talent, and create a pool of loyal employees.
- **It takes too long to administer**
  - o All plans will have some administration. The basic start-up plans might take 10 minutes to fill-out a form, 15 minutes to decide how you want to invest that money, and another 15 minutes to set-up the payroll in QuickBooks! It really is that easy. I have dealt with business owners who felt foolish because for years they were afraid to do anything, now they

realized they could have set this up in an hour and started saving for their retirement years ago. The more complex retirement plans do take more time, but by that time you are willing to pay the cost and do the upfront work for a large payoff.

- The stock market is too risky
    - I won't get into how a pool of companies that qualify to be listed on an exchange is riskier than a solo business. The key thing to remember with the stock market is that it evolves as business evolves, the success behind the market is that the companies that move the needle are the ones that have the greatest impact on the economy. What moved the economy a century ago is certainly different than the companies now. Innovative companies thrive and those that fail to innovate get delisted. The market is a living, breathing mechanism that helps to invest money in companies that matter.
    - If that doesn't sway you then you have more than just the stock market to invest in. You can invest in bonds, cash, gold, oil, silver and even annuities. Everyone has their own belief and if you decide to go away from investing in other companies than you have that option. Since it is still going in a retirement account you will get the tax benefit.

I think it is important to address any of those concerns immediately. If you have any further concerns or reasons that you can't invest in a retirement plan please let me know. I can be reached at mmeyers@ignitedaboutfinances.com. Everyone can have excuses, it is when you get past the excuses that your world really starts to open. After all excuses sound best to those who make them.

You are a big deal, you are a small business owner, you help to move the gauge on the economy, you move innovation forward. It is time for you start acting like the big deal you are.

Please read-Important for all plans

As you are reading this please keep in mind that almost all plans will have additional limits if you have a retirement plan elsewhere. If you work for yourself part-time and have a 401(k) at your full-time position, this will limit your ability to save in other retirement accounts. There are also limits on switching plans in the middle of the year. While you can start a plan in the middle of the year, if you decide to switch to a completely different plan you may not be allowed to contribute. Please consult with your financial advisor or accountant should you have any questions.

The IRS has a form 8881 that allows you to take a tax credit of $500 for the first three years of a plan. Many of these plans have minimal cost to start and much of that can be offset by the tax credit. Please inform your accountant of any start-up cost to see if they are eligible for the tax credit.

Optimism is the faith that leads to achievement. Nothing can be done without hope and confidence-Helen Keller

Traditional IRA and Roth IRA

Read if:

- *Sole proprietor just starting off*
- *Looking to make a small contribution for the year*
- *Don't have any employees that you want to provide a retirement plan for*
- *Looking for an additional way to save money*
- *Want to understand the difference between a Traditional and Roth account*

Skip if:

- *You want to provide a retirement program for your employees*
- *You don't have any additional contributions that you want to make*

It is always best to start off with the basics. If you just started a business and maybe you have a little money rolling in but you can't put a lot of money away, a lot of time just start with an IRA.

You have two basic IRA's, the Traditional and Roth IRA. The Traditional IRA is pre-taxed, which means that when you contribute into a Traditional IRA it reduces your taxable income for the year. Since the IRS wants to get that tax revenue, this is a tax-deferred vehicle. This means that when you take a distribution out of the account it is taxed at your current tax-rate. Possibly being decades down the road we don't know what that rate will be, but it does shelter taxes during that entire time.

The Roth IRA is post-taxed, which means you already paid taxes on the money that you are contributing. Since you already paid the taxes, the money grows tax-free. If you leave the money in there for the next 30 years and it grows fivefold, you can take distributions tax-free!

- Plans are easy to set-up and can be done up until the tax filing deadline (generally April 15th, no extensions allowed)
- Traditional IRA can be tax-deductible
- Roth IRA provides tax-free income for retirement
- Roth IRA doesn't have an age restriction, you can contribute if you have earned income
- No RMD (required minimum distribution) required for the Roth
- Income limitations for the Roth (can still do a back-door Roth)
- Small annual limits for contributing. Currently $5,500 plus an additional $1,000 if 50 or older
- Can have another retirement plan. This will impact your ability to deduct your contribution. Check with you advisor on how to complete a back-door Roth through a conversion.
- Roth's also have several benefits for taking distributions:
  - Can withdraw principal amount at any time without penalty (5 year holding period for money contributed via conversion)
  - First time home purchase ($10,000)
  - Medical expenses (exceeding 10% of AGI)
  - Paying medical insurance after losing job
  - Qualified higher education expenses
  - More....

The only thing worse than starting something and failing...is not starting something- Seth Godin, founder Squidoo

SEP (Simplified Employee Pension) IRA

Read if:

- *Sole proprietor just starting out*
- *Have employees, but less than three years of experience*
- *Still need to make a deduction for last year and you haven't filed your taxes*

Skip This:

- *Have multiple employees with tenure over three years*
- *You want to allow your employees to make contributions*
- *Want a Roth option for your plan*
- *Have a lot of deductions but still want to maximize your retirement contributions*

The SEP IRA is the first retirement plan for a lot of sole proprietors. The reason behind it is in its simplicity. The plan is very basic in how it is established. You can call almost any brokerage firm and they will have forms for you to establish a SEP IRA. Some basics items to keep in mind when it comes to the SEP IRA:

- It can be established at any time. For this reason, it is often the first retirement plan for new business owners. They will visit their accountant who tells them they need to reduce their taxes and they have up until the filing deadline (October 15th with an extension) to establish an account and make the contribution.

- The limit for 2017 is $54,000. This cannot exceed 25% of the employee's compensation and 20% of net self-employment income.
- If you have any employees that are 21 year old, make at least $600, and have worked with you 3 of the last 5 years than you must contribute to a SEP for them. The amount is the same percentage you are contributing. If you put in 20% for yourself, you must put in 20% of your employees pay into a SEP. You can exclude union employees and non-resident aliens.
    - Employees who are eligible must sign a form 5305-SEP. This isn't required to be turned into the IRS but simply informs the employees of your intent to establish SEP plan.
- The employee is not eligible to contribute their own money into the plan, it is strictly employer driven
- There isn't a vesting schedule, this means that any money you put into the employee's account automatically belongs to them.
- All contributions are pre-tax, this means it lowers your taxable income for the year and is taxed as income upon distribution.
- Same rules as an IRA apply, if you take a distribution prior to age 59 ½ you will be taxed on that money and pay a 10% penalty
- These are set-up in brokerage accounts, that means that you will have access to a large variety of investments. This can range from individual stocks, bonds, mutual funds, ETF's, UIT's, options, and more. There will be a commission with

each transaction so to maximize your return you will want to limit the commission cost. If all the choices are confusing work with an advisor who can develop a plan for you. The extra cost upfront pays dividends down the road.

The SEP IRA is an easy way to reduce your taxable income and save a large amount of money. While you can have employees and still establish a SEP, most owners will steer away from that. The reason is that they want employees to have "skin" in the game and make their own contributions. This could also limit the owner to a matching percentage. If they contribute a large percentage of their salary they wouldn't have the obligation to contribute a large amount to their employees.

With the being said, I still see SEP accounts established with employees, especially when it is family run. Owners tend to be a little more generous when it comes to their family. If it a cash flow positive venture than why not share the wealth, literally.

Risk more than others think is safe. Dream more than others think is practical- Howard Schultz, Starbucks CEO

Solo 401(k)

Read if:

- *It is just yourself or you and your spouse, and you have no full-time employees (1000 hours a year)*
- *You have a lot of deductions but still want to maximize your deferrals*
- *Want a Traditional (tax-deferred) or Roth (tax-free) option*

Skip this:

- *You have any full-time employees*

This is also known as an individual 401(k). If you are working by yourself than this is a great product. The advantages of a 401(k) are well known and the flexibility with the program makes it a winner.

- To qualify you can't have any full-time employees, with an exception being your spouse. You can have part-time employees (less than 1000 hours ayear) and contractors. Once you get a full-time employee you must terminate your plan or move it to a regular 401(k).
- The 401(k) option allows for both Traditional 401(k) contributions which reduce your taxable income, and Roth 401(k) contributions which are tax-free at normal distribution of 59 ½.

- With a 401(k) you can deduct 100% of your salary as an elective deferral up to the limits, which is currently $18,000 in 2017, $24,000 if you are 50 or older. Elective deferral refers to the amount as an "employee" you are contributing. You can also match yourself as the employer. The first few years may be lean, with a 401(K) you can, possibly, contribute a larger percentage of your salary instead of the 20% limit on SEP's.

- You can also provide a match. The match along with your elective contributions cannot exceed $54,000 ($60,000 if you are 50 or older). All matches must be done into a Traditional 401(k), while elective deferrals can be done in either.

- Non-elective contributions are limited to 25% of compensation. This is easier to calculate if you decide to W-2 yourself. If you go strictly off self-employment income than there is a calculation that is required, this would be close to 20% net income. You can also use IRS publication 560 to get a precise number, or consult with your accountant.

- There is an income limitation on the match, which is $270,000. That means if you made $350,000 and you match 50% up to 5% than only $270,000 of income could be considered for the match (50%(5%x$270,000)) which would limit the match to $6,750.

- Like regular 401(k)'s you can set-up a solo 401(k) so you can take loans against the balance. Please keep in mind that anytime you add options like this you add to the cost of the plan.

- It used to be expensive to administer a solo 401(k), that has changed. Many places offer a template at no cost to set-up a plan. Many of these providers will charge a commission for the product purchased inside the plan.

- Other providers will use a vendor and charge a nominal fee to set-up the plan, once the plan is set-up look for someone who has a list of no-fee mutual funds. This makes the 401(k) advantageous and cost effective.
- If you ever looked at a 401(k) there is talk about non-discrimination testing, you don't have to worry about that if you don't have any employees. In addition, you don't have to file the form 5500 with the IRS at the end of the year. Talk about easy. If the assets in your plan do exceed $250,000 you will have to fill out a form 5500-EZ which is simplified for solo 401(k)'s. If you don't want to deal with the paperwork the IRS has a form 5500-SF that you can complete right online, this is a "short form" of the form 5500.
- You must sign-up by December of the year you are making contributions. If you want to make contribution in 2017, you must have the account established in 2017. You can make a lump sum or contributions throughout the year. The actual contribution into the plan can be made, up to, your tax filing deadline.

The solo 401(k) offers some big benefits over the SEP IRA and brokerage firms are making it easier to sign-up. Take advantage of the no-fee mutual funds, the ability to put away 100% of your income and the option to invest in a Roth. If you want additional bells and whistles such as the ability to take a loan out on your balance you will find that option is available as well.

The solo 401(k) offers the advantages that larger companies have with their 401(k) without the additional administrative cost. If you want to remain a solo practitioner, you may find putting your spouse on the payroll makes sense for your situation to save additional money into retirement.

SIMPLE (Savings Incentive Match Plan for Employee's Individual Retirement Account) IRA

Read if:

- *You want almost all employees to be eligible to contribute*
- *You have a lot of deductions but want to save some money toward retirement*
- *Looking for a tax-deduction*
- *Have less than 100 employees*

Skip this:

- *You want a Roth option*
- *You want to contribute more than $15,000 per year*
- *You want a loan option*
- *You want to limit who can participate in the plan*

Thank goodness for acronyms. The SIMPLE is a basic plan that is easy to set-up, and easy to operate. Based on the premise that business owners want a plan where their employees can contribute and receive a match without the administrative cost of a 401(k).

- To qualify you must have 100 or fewer employees who made $5,000 during the preceding year. All employees who worked during the calendar year are included. Companies can exclude union employees and non-resident aliens.
- Plans must be established by October 1st of the year you are making contributions.

- o Employee elective deferrals must be made within 30 days after the end of the month in which the amounts would otherwise have been made payable.
  - o Employer matches or contributions must be made by the tax filing deadline.
- Employee must reasonably expect to make $5,000 to qualify, there aren't any age restrictions with this plan.
- Employer and employee will complete a for 5305-SIMPLE. This states that the employee is eligible for the plan, they are aware of enrollment, and they have decided to defer money or decline.
  - o There is also a form 5304-SIMPLE. This is if the employees can select their own financial institution to house their SIMPLE. I haven't seen an employee make this decision, because if you are sending in a check to a company do you want to make it one check to one place, or try to send multiple checks to several companies, most would choose the former. However, the option is there and this form allows the employee to tell the employer where to send the check.
- Two ways that you can make a match within the plan
  - o 2% non-elective contribution-This means you contribute 2% of the employee's salary into the SIMPLE plan regardless of whether they contributed.
  - o 3% matching contribution-This means you match an employee's contribution dollar-for-dollar up to 3% of their salary
    - ▪ Should you come across tough times you can reduce the match to no lower than 1% for two calendar years in the last five.
- Employees must be given a 60-day enrollment window to participate, however employers can offer more generous terms for enrolling and changing contribution levels.

- Employees can stop their contributions at any time.
- No discrimination testing, or forms that must be filed.
- Employees can defer $12,500, plus an additional $3,000 if you are 50 or older. All contributions are tax-deferred, the Roth option is not available with the SIMPLE IRA.
- Distributions are a little more restrictive for SIMPLE IRA's. If a distribution is made within the first two years of opening the SIMPLE that is not qualified (age 59 ½) than a 25% penalty is imposed in addition to the withdrawal taxed as income.
- Most firms will set these up in brokerage accounts, this means a commission is charged for each transaction
- No vesting schedule, any matches made into the plan are the employees

When it comes to simplicity it is hard to pass up the SIMPLE IRA. For a company of 75 employees they could set this up with relative ease and there would be little administrative cost outside of the initial set-up. The downside to the SIMPLE is the inability to put away a lot of money like you can with a 401(k) plan. This plan is limited to the traditional pre-tax offering. In addition, if you are looking for extras like loans you will not find that with this plan.

The ability to put more money away is usually felt hardest by the owner of the plan. This is a great gateway plan to a traditional 401(k). Without any annual filing, TPA cost, or forms to file it can reduce the burden on a business owner who doesn't have a large support staff in place. As the business grows and becomes more profitable the owner can switch to a 401(k) when they are ready.

Our customers get it. They know they'll get a better job done because everyone out here is a part owner of the company. That means we've all got more pride in our work. We'll do our best and everything we can to make sure that customer is a customer again. And again. The thing is, we're not just working for someone else, we're working for ourselves- Ray Atkinson

Profit Sharing/Money Purchase Programs

Read if:

- *Looking for an additional method to save for retirement*
- *Want employees to share in the profitability of the company*

Skip this:

- *Don't want to deal with administrative cost*
- *Don't want another retirement option (this can act as a standalone)*

These plans are often used in correlation with a 401(k) plan, even though they can be used as a standalone. The idea behind both plans is to share part of the businesses profits with employees. Incentivizing employee's by sharing in the company's profits, you tend to find a more engaged workforce, a workforce that is looking to cut cost, and doing what they can to increase productivity and profits.

The only difference between a profit-sharing and money purchase plan is the requirement to contribute to the employees. With a profit-sharing plan there isn't an obligation, this can help a business that must deal with the ebbs and flows of their business cycle. Some years they will be able to contribute, other years they can opt out. With a money purchase plans, contributions are required by a certain percentage specified in the plan documents.

- To qualify an employee must be 21 years of age, worked at least one year (two years if 100% vesting), and work more than 1000 hours. A company can exclude union employees and nonresident aliens.
- A vesting schedule is allowed. This provides an incentive for the employees to stay with the company so they don't forfeit their unvested portion.
- Can have other retirement plans.
- Completely employer driven contributions.
- Need to annually file the form 5500.
- Loans may be allowed.
- Can contribute 25% of compensation, up to $54,000. This is limited to 20% of net income for self-employed filing.
- Must be established for the plan year end that you intend to make the contribution for tax filings (December 31st in most cases), actual contribution can be made up until the tax filing deadline.

These plans can be set-up for small companies or large ones. There is a benefit to letting the employees that if certain benchmarks are hit for the year they can expect a bonus. Instead of a company simply having employees show-up to their jobs, they now have engaged employees working toward a common goal.

Another advantage to profit-sharing plans is that they allow for cross-tested plans. This allows the business owner to allocate a higher contribution rate to themselves and other highly compensated employees. There is a gateway amount they must provide for the employees, think of this as a toll, once that threshold is met, then the owner can place the rest toward the business owner and highly compensated employees.

There are several rules with this testing. An ideal situation would be a large age and income discrepancy between the employer and employees. This would provide the optimum benefit for the owner.

There are multiple ways to set these up, discuss this with your TPA to find out which one is most appropriate for your business.

Employees are a company's greatest asset- they're your competitive advantage. You want to attract and retain the best; provide them with encouragement, stimulus, and make them feel that they are an integral part of the company's mission- Anne M. Mulcahy

401(k)/403(b) Plans

Read if:

- *Looking to defer a significant amount of money into retirement account*
- *Want to create an incentive for employees to stay with the company*
- *Want a Roth (tax-free) option for saving*
- *Want to borrow against your balance (optional)*
- *Have a large base of employees who could contribute*

Skip this:

- *Don't want to deal with administrative cost and restrictions associated with Traditional 401(k)*
- *You're looking to defer less than $15,000 and have less than 100 employees*

We will review both the 401(k) and the 403(b) since they are similar. The limitations are the same across the board. There will be a couple of main differences. The first is that 403(b) plans generally don't have limitations on who can contribute to the plan. If you are working with a non-profit 501(c)(3) organization than you will be eligible to contribute to the plan. A 401(k) plan will typically require 1 year of work, be 21 years of age, and work full-time. The other difference is that 403(b) plans are geared toward non-profits, these plans are most common in schools, hospitals, governments, and other organizations. In the discussion, I will mention 401(k) generically, include 403(b) plans.

The 401(k) plan is the direction that businesses are going. The 401(k) allows for employees to take control of their retirement and for the company to assist in that process. The days of guaranteed pensions are going away for most governments and businesses. Institutions can no longer burden themselves with the obligation required under traditional pension plans. As global competition continues, more companies are unwilling to commit to a set amount of money, given that their business model could change dramatically. Smart companies are using retirement plans to lure in quality talent. The ADP Research Institute found that 80% of employees view a retirement plan as a key consideration when looking at employers. Currently only 50% of businesses offer some sort of retirement plan.

- Plans must be established by December 31st of the tax year you are making contributions
- Can set-up automatic enrollment, this means that employees must opt-out instead of opting into the plan, must set-up 3% employee contribution in their first year
- A vesting schedule is permitted for employer matches.
- A match is not required in the plan (unless automatic enrollment)
- Loans may be allowed.
- Employees can defer $18,000, an additional $6,000 is permitted if they are 50 or older.
- Total employee/employer contributions cannot exceed $54,000 plus $6,000 if 50 or older
- Employer contribution is limited to 25% of compensation up to $270,000
- Self-employment compensation is limited to approximately 20% of net income

- Employee and employer compensation
- Must file form 5500 annually.
- Subject to discrimination testing

A 401(k) is a great program with flexibility and the ability to put away significant money. If you go with a traditional 401(k) the plan will be tested every year by a TPA (third party administrator). Their job is to make sure that the plan complies with all the rules and regulations and keep you safe. The discrimination testing is done to ensure that everyone is participating in the plan and it is a way to promote the plan to employees

The plan will look at HCE's (highly compensated employees). This includes any owners of the business that own more than 5% regardless of their pay in the past year. This also includes employees who made at least $120,000 in 2017. If more than 60% of the plan assets fall within HCE's than further testing is required.

This is a test referred to as ACP (actual contribution percentage test), this compares the average percentage of matching contributions and after-tax employee contributions for HCE's and NHCE's (non-highly compensated employees). In addition, there is a similar test called the ADP (actual deferral percentage), this test looks at actual deferral percentages and does not consider matching. These tests are best illustrated, basically there are limitations on how much HCE's can contribute base on the average of NHCE's. The IRS has these limits based on the contribution percentage of employees.

NHCE Percentage	Maximum HCE Percentage
2% or less	NHCE% X 2
2%-8%	NHCE% + 2
More than 8%	NHCE% X 1.25

Above illustrates the maximum amount a HCE could put away based on the NHCE. Per the IRS guidelines if the average amount put away was just 2%, HCE could put two times that amount away, so just 4%. If NHCE put away 9% of their income, an HCE could put away 11.25% of their income away, there is an incentive to encourage meaningful participation.

Employee	Compensation	Deferral	ADP
HCE 1	$ 250,000.00	$ 12,500.00	5.0%
HCE 2	$ 120,000.00	$ 12,000.00	10.0%
Total			15.0%
Average			7.5%
NHCE 1	$ 40,000.00	$ 4,000.00	10.0%
NHCE 2	$ 35,000.00	$ -	0.0%
NHCE 3	$ 35,000.00	$ 2,000.00	5.7%
NHCE 4	$ 30,000.00	$ 2,500.00	8.3%
NHCE 5	$ 30,000.00	$ 3,000.00	10.0%
Total			34.0%
Average			6.8%

In the above example since the average for NHCE is 6.8%, this would allow HCE to put up to 8.8% of their compensation away without violating the guidelines. In this case, they are complying and no action is required.

What if the plan was found in violation in the above case? The plan must take corrective action and rectify the problem generally within 2 ½ months after the end of the plan year. The most common solution is for the HCE's to have an excess distribution taken out of their account. This is a taxable event (they already got the tax break) and is reported on a form 1099-R. Any matches made up to the amount they contributed in excess are forfeited back to the company.

A second solution is to make a broad contribution in the NHCE's accounts to bring their total percentage up to the required amount. The same percentage must be given to everyone. This solution is rarely used but should a company be very close, it would be a feasible option.

Once the first year of the plan is complete, it is easier for the company to use the prior year's results to make an educated guess on how much HCE's can contribute. As more years of results are calculated the company can make decisions with some reliability as to how much HCE's can save.

The penalty for not taking corrective action is severe. In some cases, the 401(k) plan could lose its tax preferential status. If the company did not take corrective action, the company can also be fined 10% of the excess contributions made into the plan. If you are working with a trusted TPA they should see the warning signs and help you to take corrective action ahead of time. The government wants you to save and help your employees save, they allow plenty of time for corrective action and most of the time that simply isn't necessary.

Never overlook the power of simplicity- Robin S Sharma

Safe Harbor 401(k) Plans

Read if:

- *You read the restrictions on a Traditional 401(k) and you don't want to deal with it*
- *You want to attract quality employees with an attractive match*
- *You want to maximize your retirement deferrals*
- *You want a Roth option*
- *You want to borrow against your balance (optional)*

Skip this:

- *Don't want to deal with administrative cost*
- *You want to restrict matches with a vesting schedule*

If you read the information about 401(k)'s and you are thinking "what a hassle", you aren't alone. The reality is that when it comes to small businesses the owner tends to have the most assets and that can be an issue when it comes to testing your plan. The brunt of the consequences falls on the business owner and they would prefer to run their business instead of deal with 401(k) paperwork.

That is why many small business owners are opening safe harbor 401(k) plans. These plans automatically pass the ADP/ACP and top-heavy test. This allows a business owner to maximize the contributions to their plan without fear of negative consequences.

The contribution limits are the same as a 401(k) but there are a few key differences:

- You must offer a match to the employees and that match is 100% vested, most traditional 401(k) plans will have a six-year vesting schedule
- Two types of matches:
  - Basic match-100% match on the first 3% of deferred compensation plus a 50% for deferrals between 3% and 5% (4% total)
  - Enhanced match-must be at least as much as the basic match, a common match is a 100% on the first 4% of deferred compensation.
- There is also a non-elective contribution option available. This is a flat 3% match across the board regardless of whether participants contribute to the plan.

With all the non-discrimination testing required in a 401(k), a safe harbor plan can provide peace of mind to employers letting them know they can maximize their 401(k) without having to worry about employee deferrals.

Defined Benefit Plans

Read if:

- *You want to provide a guaranteed benefit to your employees*
- *Your company has enough predictable cash flow to make continuous ongoing contributions*
- *You want loyal employees for years*
- *You want retirement options for different classes of workers*
- *You want more than one retirement plan*

Skip this:

- *Have an unpredictable revenue stream*
- *Want to avoid the costliest retirement plan*
- *Don't want to be subject to the market swings in your contribution amount*

These are the pension plans that everyone in large corporations were promised years ago. This is also the reason that you had employees who would work for the same company for decades. The defined benefit plan spells out exactly what your benefit will be when you retire based on a formula. This formula calculates your length of service and salary when you retired. For example, the plan may promise $125 per month, times your number of years of services, if you worked for the company for 20 years your benefit would be $2,500. The onus is on the company to provide that benefit.

Because the company is responsible for paying the benefits they must have an actuary sign off on the form 5500 every single year. In addition, there are a myriad of rules that need to be followed under the Employee Retirement Income Security Act of 1974 (ERISA) and the Internal Revenue Code. For this reason, they are expensive to operate and require the expertise of a good TPA (third party administrator).

Some key points with Defined Benefit Plans:

- You can have other retirements plans
- Can't decrease past benefits
- Vesting schedules are allowed
- Most costly plan
    - Administratively complex
    - Employees can accrue substantial benefits in a short period of time
- Penalized if a company contributes too much or too little into the plan
- Secure feeling for employees
- Most benefits are insured, up to a limit, by the federal government through the Pension Benefit Guaranty Corporation (PBGC)
- Up to the company to bring the plan up to its funding level, even if the stock market and economy is down.
- Offer a single life annuity, joint life annuity at retirement, or lump sum at retirement

These plans have been replaced, in many cases, by 401(k) and other defined contribution plans. Companies are looking for ways in which they can provide a benefit for their employees but not be held liable for market returns and business cycles. However, there are cases where these can make sense for a business and provide a guaranteed benefit for your employees. This benefit does encourage employees to stick around, many times, for decades.

Defined Contribution Plan

This is a retirement plan in which either a set dollar amount or set percentage is contributed to a plan on behalf of employees. While this is more synonymous with 401(K) plans, this also includes TSP plans, SIMPLE's, money purchase pension, and ESOP's (employee stock option plans). Since so much of the language it thrown around it is important to understand that some of the language just describes how the plans operate. When you hear defined contribution plan, just remember this is describing one of the retirement plans where a company contribute a set amount.

The only person who will take care of the older person you will someday be, is the younger person you are now-Unknown

How Much Should I Save?

This is a common question that I get and one that doesn't have an easy answer. This is where the vagueness of financial planning frustrates people who want an easy answer. The reality is that the answer depends on what stage of life you are in, when you want to retire, and what life style you want to retire with.

A big factor that people forget to consider is the "fear" factor. This is the fear of losing money in the marketplace. This is known as loss aversion, in other words the idea of losing $1,000 is more powerful than finding $1,000. This impedes the ability of individuals to invest successfully for the long-term. Individuals will react with recent news and irrationally make predictions on short-term events. For example, an official being elected, a terrorist act, a declaration of war, recession, or other news events. Instead of sticking with a balanced investment strategy

Instead of sticking with a plan they end up selling low, buying high, or simply putting money in a low interest-bearing account. Part of the equation of how much you should save depends on how much risk you are willing to take with your investments. While I can appreciate the fear of losing money, I've seen too many people stick their money in investments that cause them to lose money to inflation every year. Inflation is simply an increase in prices and a fall in the purchasing value of money.

In the graph below it show $50,000 invested in 4 different investments. The first is a "safe" savings account earning .1% with inflation at a steady 2.5%. Under this scenario after 30 years you have half of the purchasing power compared to when you originally deposited the money. The other show progressively more aggressive amounts and the impact of compounding interest at higher rates.

Retirement Plans Made Simple

Year	Current 1%	Inflation 2.5%	Buying Power	Income 4%	Inflation 2.5%	Buying Power	Conservative 6%	Inflation	Buying Power	Growth 8%	Inflation	Buying Power
1	$50,050.00	$51,250.00	97.7%	$52,000.00	$51,250.00	101.5%	$53,000.00	$51,250.00	103.4%	$54,000.00	$51,250.00	105.4%
2	$50,100.05	$52,531.25	95.4%	$54,080.00	$52,531.25	102.9%	$56,180.00	$52,531.25	106.9%	$58,320.00	$52,531.25	111.0%
3	$50,150.15	$53,844.53	93.1%	$56,243.20	$53,844.53	104.5%	$59,550.80	$53,844.53	110.6%	$62,985.60	$53,844.53	117.0%
4	$50,200.30	$55,190.64	91.0%	$58,492.93	$55,190.64	106.0%	$63,123.85	$55,190.64	114.4%	$68,024.45	$55,190.64	123.3%
5	$50,250.50	$56,570.41	88.8%	$60,832.65	$56,570.41	107.5%	$66,911.28	$56,570.41	118.3%	$73,466.40	$56,570.41	129.9%
6	$50,300.75	$57,984.67	86.7%	$63,265.95	$57,984.67	109.1%	$70,925.96	$57,984.67	122.3%	$79,343.72	$57,984.67	136.8%
7	$50,351.05	$59,434.29	84.7%	$65,796.59	$59,434.29	110.7%	$75,181.51	$59,434.29	126.5%	$85,691.21	$59,434.29	144.2%
8	$50,401.40	$60,920.14	82.7%	$68,428.45	$60,920.14	112.3%	$79,692.40	$60,920.14	130.8%	$92,546.51	$60,920.14	151.9%
9	$50,451.80	$62,443.15	80.8%	$71,165.59	$62,443.15	114.0%	$84,473.95	$62,443.15	135.3%	$99,950.23	$62,443.15	160.1%
10	$50,502.26	$64,004.23	78.9%	$74,012.21	$64,004.23	115.6%	$89,542.38	$64,004.23	139.9%	$107,946.25	$64,004.23	168.7%
11	$50,552.76	$65,604.33	77.1%	$76,972.70	$65,604.33	117.3%	$94,914.93	$65,604.33	144.7%	$116,581.95	$65,604.33	177.7%
12	$50,603.31	$67,244.44	75.3%	$80,051.61	$67,244.44	119.0%	$100,609.82	$67,244.44	149.6%	$125,908.51	$67,244.44	187.2%
13	$50,653.91	$68,925.55	73.5%	$83,253.68	$68,925.55	120.8%	$106,646.41	$68,925.55	154.7%	$135,981.19	$68,925.55	197.3%
14	$50,704.57	$70,648.69	71.8%	$86,583.82	$70,648.69	122.6%	$113,045.20	$70,648.69	160.0%	$146,859.68	$70,648.69	207.9%
15	$50,755.27	$72,414.91	70.1%	$90,047.18	$72,414.91	124.3%	$119,827.91	$72,414.91	165.5%	$158,608.46	$72,414.91	219.0%
16	$50,806.03	$74,225.28	68.4%	$93,649.06	$74,225.28	126.2%	$127,017.58	$74,225.28	171.1%	$171,297.13	$74,225.28	230.8%
17	$50,856.83	$76,080.91	66.8%	$97,395.02	$76,080.91	128.0%	$134,638.64	$76,080.91	177.0%	$185,000.90	$76,080.91	243.2%
18	$50,907.69	$77,982.94	65.3%	$101,290.83	$77,982.94	129.9%	$142,716.96	$77,982.94	183.0%	$199,800.97	$77,982.94	256.2%
19	$50,958.60	$79,932.51	63.8%	$105,342.46	$79,932.51	131.8%	$151,279.98	$79,932.51	189.3%	$215,785.05	$79,932.51	270.0%
20	$51,009.56	$81,930.82	62.3%	$109,556.16	$81,930.82	133.7%	$160,356.77	$81,930.82	195.7%	$233,047.86	$81,930.82	284.4%
21	$51,060.57	$83,979.09	60.8%	$113,938.40	$83,979.09	135.7%	$169,978.18	$83,979.09	202.4%	$251,691.69	$83,979.09	299.7%
22	$51,111.63	$86,078.57	59.4%	$118,495.94	$86,078.57	137.7%	$180,176.87	$86,078.57	209.3%	$271,827.02	$86,078.57	315.8%
23	$51,162.74	$88,230.53	58.0%	$123,235.78	$88,230.53	139.7%	$190,987.48	$88,230.53	216.5%	$293,573.18	$88,230.53	332.7%
24	$51,213.90	$90,436.30	56.6%	$128,165.21	$90,436.30	141.7%	$202,446.73	$90,436.30	223.9%	$317,059.04	$90,436.30	350.6%
25	$51,265.12	$92,697.20	55.3%	$133,291.82	$92,697.20	143.8%	$214,593.54	$92,697.20	231.5%	$342,423.76	$92,697.20	369.4%
26	$51,316.38	$95,014.64	54.0%	$138,623.49	$95,014.64	145.9%	$227,469.15	$95,014.64	239.4%	$369,817.66	$95,014.64	389.2%
27	$51,367.70	$97,390.00	52.7%	$144,168.43	$97,390.00	148.0%	$241,117.30	$97,390.00	247.6%	$399,403.07	$97,390.00	410.1%
28	$51,419.06	$99,824.75	51.5%	$149,935.17	$99,824.75	150.2%	$255,584.33	$99,824.75	256.0%	$431,355.32	$99,824.75	432.1%
29	$51,470.48	$102,320.37	50.3%	$155,932.57	$102,320.37	152.4%	$270,919.39	$102,320.37	264.8%	$465,863.74	$102,320.37	455.3%
30	$51,521.95	$104,878.38	49.1%	$162,169.88	$104,878.38	154.6%	$287,174.56	$104,878.38	273.8%	$503,132.84	$104,878.38	479.7%

The more time and more aggressive you can be with your investments the more successful your outcome.

The next factor is how much you need to save. To do that you will want to calculate your current cost and project them into retirement. The further you are away from retirement the more difficult this will be. We are dealing with a lot of variables but planning is going to be the key, you can always adjust as you get closer to retirement. If you haven't put together a budget or you're aren't sure where to start, please check out my book *Ignited About Crushing Debt* for more information.

Below are two charts, these illustrate what saving money at a 4% rate of return compared to an 8% return. I realize that getting a straight-line return on your investments like this isn't realistic, but it does give an indication of how powerful a few percent can make. In addition, this should give you an idea of how much you can save. Many of the plans allow you to save upwards of $50,000 per year, if you are aggressive you can save much more than what is illustrated. The distribution amount is assumed at 4%, this amount will also vary based on age and other factors.

Year	$10K 4% Return	Contribution	Approximate Distribution	$10K 8% Return	Contribution	Approximate Distribution
1	$ 10,000.00	$ 10,000.00	$ 400.00	$ 10,000.00	$ 10,000.00	$ 400.00
2	$ 21,112.00	$ 10,300.00	$ 844.48	$ 21,924.00	$ 10,300.00	$ 876.96
3	$ 32,989.84	$ 10,609.00	$ 1,319.59	$ 35,135.64	$ 10,609.00	$ 1,405.43
4	$ 45,673.79	$ 10,927.27	$ 1,826.95	$ 49,747.94	$ 10,927.27	$ 1,989.92
5	$ 59,206.04	$ 11,255.09	$ 2,368.24	$ 65,883.27	$ 11,255.09	$ 2,635.33
6	$ 73,630.73	$ 11,592.74	$ 2,945.23	$ 83,674.10	$ 11,592.74	$ 3,346.96
7	$ 88,994.10	$ 11,940.52	$ 3,559.76	$ 103,263.79	$ 11,940.52	$ 4,130.55
8	$ 105,344.56	$ 12,298.74	$ 4,213.78	$ 124,807.53	$ 12,298.74	$ 4,992.30
9	$ 122,732.75	$ 12,667.70	$ 4,909.31	$ 148,473.25	$ 12,667.70	$ 5,938.93
10	$ 141,211.70	$ 13,047.73	$ 5,648.47	$ 174,442.66	$ 13,047.73	$ 6,977.71
11	$ 160,836.90	$ 13,439.16	$ 6,433.48	$ 202,912.37	$ 13,439.16	$ 8,116.49
12	$ 181,666.40	$ 13,842.34	$ 7,266.66	$ 234,095.08	$ 13,842.34	$ 9,363.80
13	$ 203,760.97	$ 14,257.61	$ 8,150.44	$ 268,220.91	$ 14,257.61	$ 10,728.84
14	$ 227,184.16	$ 14,685.34	$ 9,087.37	$ 305,538.74	$ 14,685.34	$ 12,221.55
15	$ 252,002.46	$ 15,125.90	$ 10,080.10	$ 346,317.81	$ 15,125.90	$ 13,852.71
16	$ 278,285.42	$ 15,579.67	$ 11,131.42	$ 390,849.28	$ 15,579.67	$ 15,633.97
17	$ 306,105.79	$ 16,047.06	$ 12,244.23	$ 439,448.06	$ 16,047.06	$ 17,577.92
18	$ 335,539.63	$ 16,528.48	$ 13,421.59	$ 492,454.66	$ 16,528.48	$ 19,698.19
19	$ 366,666.52	$ 17,024.33	$ 14,666.66	$ 550,237.31	$ 17,024.33	$ 22,009.49
20	$ 399,569.65	$ 17,535.06	$ 15,982.79	$ 613,194.16	$ 17,535.06	$ 24,527.77
21	$ 434,335.99	$ 18,061.11	$ 17,373.44	$ 681,755.69	$ 18,061.11	$ 27,270.23
22	$ 471,056.49	$ 18,602.95	$ 18,842.26	$ 756,387.33	$ 18,602.95	$ 30,255.49
23	$ 509,826.23	$ 19,161.03	$ 20,393.05	$ 837,592.23	$ 19,161.03	$ 33,503.69
24	$ 550,744.57	$ 19,735.87	$ 22,029.78	$ 925,914.34	$ 19,735.87	$ 37,036.57
25	$ 593,915.42	$ 20,327.94	$ 23,756.62	$ 1,021,941.66	$ 20,327.94	$ 40,877.67
26	$ 639,447.32	$ 20,937.78	$ 25,577.89	$ 1,126,309.80	$ 20,937.78	$ 45,052.39
27	$ 687,453.77	$ 21,565.91	$ 27,498.15	$ 1,239,705.77	$ 21,565.91	$ 49,588.23
28	$ 738,053.32	$ 22,212.89	$ 29,522.13	$ 1,362,872.15	$ 22,212.89	$ 54,514.89
29	$ 791,369.90	$ 22,879.28	$ 31,654.80	$ 1,496,611.54	$ 22,879.28	$ 59,864.46
30	$ 847,532.98	$ 23,565.66	$ 33,901.32	$ 1,641,791.37	$ 23,565.66	$ 65,671.65

Year	$20K 4% Return	Contribution	Approximate Distribution	$20K 8% Return	Contribution	Approximate Distribution
1	$ 20,000.00	$ 20,000.00	$ 800.00	$ 20,000.00	$ 20,000.00	$ 800.00
2	$ 42,224.00	$ 20,600.00	$ 1,688.96	$ 43,848.00	$ 20,600.00	$ 1,753.92
3	$ 65,979.68	$ 21,218.00	$ 2,639.19	$ 70,271.28	$ 21,218.00	$ 2,810.85
4	$ 91,347.59	$ 21,854.54	$ 3,653.90	$ 99,495.89	$ 21,854.54	$ 3,979.84
5	$ 118,412.08	$ 22,510.18	$ 4,736.48	$ 131,766.55	$ 22,510.18	$ 5,270.66
6	$ 147,261.46	$ 23,185.48	$ 5,890.46	$ 167,348.19	$ 23,185.48	$ 6,693.93
7	$ 177,988.21	$ 23,881.05	$ 7,119.53	$ 206,527.58	$ 23,881.05	$ 8,261.10
8	$ 210,689.11	$ 24,597.48	$ 8,427.56	$ 249,615.06	$ 24,597.48	$ 9,984.60
9	$ 245,465.49	$ 25,335.40	$ 9,818.62	$ 296,946.50	$ 25,335.40	$ 11,877.86
10	$ 282,423.39	$ 26,095.46	$ 11,296.94	$ 348,885.32	$ 26,095.46	$ 13,955.41
11	$ 321,673.79	$ 26,878.33	$ 12,866.95	$ 405,824.73	$ 26,878.33	$ 16,232.99
12	$ 363,332.81	$ 27,684.68	$ 14,533.31	$ 468,190.16	$ 27,684.68	$ 18,727.61
13	$ 407,521.95	$ 28,515.22	$ 16,300.88	$ 536,441.81	$ 28,515.22	$ 21,457.67
14	$ 454,368.32	$ 29,370.67	$ 18,174.73	$ 611,077.49	$ 29,370.67	$ 24,443.10
15	$ 504,004.92	$ 30,251.79	$ 20,160.20	$ 692,635.62	$ 30,251.79	$ 27,705.42
16	$ 556,570.84	$ 31,159.35	$ 22,262.83	$ 781,698.57	$ 31,159.35	$ 31,267.94
17	$ 612,211.57	$ 32,094.13	$ 24,488.46	$ 878,896.11	$ 32,094.13	$ 35,155.84
18	$ 671,079.26	$ 33,056.95	$ 26,843.17	$ 984,909.31	$ 33,056.95	$ 39,396.37
19	$ 733,333.04	$ 34,048.66	$ 29,333.32	$ 1,100,474.61	$ 34,048.66	$ 44,018.98
20	$ 799,139.29	$ 35,070.12	$ 31,965.57	$ 1,226,388.31	$ 35,070.12	$ 49,055.53
21	$ 868,671.98	$ 36,122.22	$ 34,746.88	$ 1,363,511.38	$ 36,122.22	$ 54,540.46
22	$ 942,112.98	$ 37,205.89	$ 37,684.52	$ 1,512,774.65	$ 37,205.89	$ 60,510.99
23	$ 1,019,652.45	$ 38,322.07	$ 40,786.10	$ 1,675,184.46	$ 38,322.07	$ 67,007.38
24	$ 1,101,489.15	$ 39,471.73	$ 44,059.57	$ 1,851,828.68	$ 39,471.73	$ 74,073.15
25	$ 1,187,830.83	$ 40,655.88	$ 47,513.23	$ 2,043,883.33	$ 40,655.88	$ 81,755.33
26	$ 1,278,894.65	$ 41,875.56	$ 51,155.79	$ 2,252,619.60	$ 41,875.56	$ 90,104.78
27	$ 1,374,907.53	$ 43,131.83	$ 54,996.30	$ 2,479,411.54	$ 43,131.83	$ 99,176.46
28	$ 1,476,106.64	$ 44,425.78	$ 59,044.27	$ 2,725,744.30	$ 44,425.78	$ 109,029.77
29	$ 1,582,739.80	$ 45,758.55	$ 63,309.59	$ 2,993,223.09	$ 45,758.55	$ 119,728.92
30	$ 1,695,065.96	$ 47,131.31	$ 67,802.64	$ 3,283,582.75	$ 47,131.31	$ 131,343.31

Your best solution is to take the time to sit down with an advisor and come-up with specific options regarding your circumstances. An advisor would be able to look at your whole situation, incorporate social security, pensions, permanent life insurance, and other income into your situation. If your business has profits that swing wildly from year-to-year they would be able to come-up with solutions for that.

Retirement plans provide a vehicle to reduce your taxable income, shelter taxes, and potentially provide for a tax-free account. The more you can utilize these vehicles the quicker you can build wealth outside of your business. Take advantage of every deduction you can to provide yourself a better tomorrow.

The key is to be aggressive in how much you save and be willing to take on some risk to make the money grow. I have never met someone who said they were upset because they saved too much. If anything, it gave them options when they retired on how they wished to spend their golden years.

Most common Plans for Sole Proprietors and Companies With a Few Employees-2017 Data

Plan	Limits	Benefits	Restrictions	Contribution Deadline	Plan Administration	Established Deadline
Roth IRA	$5,500 plus an additiona $1,000 if 50 or older	Tax-free growth, contributions after age 70 1/2	Income restrictions, can do a conversion from Traditional IRA	Tax filing deadline, no extensions	None	Tax filing deadline, no extensions
Traditional IRA	$5,500 plus an additiona $1,000 if 50 or older	May be tax-deductible, used w/other retirement plans	age limit of 70 1/2, deductibility if in a retirement plan	Tax filing deadline, no extensions	None	Tax filing deadline, no extensions
Solo 401(k)	$18,000 + $6,000 if 50 or older. Match + deferrals cannot exceed $54,000 +$6,000 for those 50 or older	Tax-free, or tax-deferred growth. Loans may be available. Non-commission mutual funds	Only Owner and spouse allowed on plan	For business owners, when salary income is determined, tax-filing deadline + extensions	Minimal, generally a single form with Solo 401(k)'s (No TPA)	December 31st of the year you want to make the contributions
SIMPLE IRA	$12,500 + $3,000 if 50 or older	Tax-deferred growth, pre-tax contributions. No TPA administrative cost	Companies with 100 employees or fewer.	Salary deferral on pay period, employer contributions by tax deadline plus extension	None	October 1st of the year you want to make contributions
SEP IRA	25% of compensation up to $54,000, approximately 20% for sole proprietors	Employer-funded, easy to establish and maintain.	Age 21, worked three of the last five years and made at least $600	Tax filing deadline plus extensions	None	Tax filing deadline plus extensions

Most common Plans for Advanced Companies With 10 or more Employees-2017 Data

Plan	Limits	Benefits	Restrictions	Contribution Deadline	Plan Administration	Established Deadline
Profit Sharing/Money Purchase	25% of compensation up to $54,000, approximately 20% for sole proprietors. PSP are discretionary, MPP are required	Allows for a vesting schedule, restrictions on coverage, may allow for loans	Age 21 or older, worked 1 year with company (2 years if 100% vested). Can exclude part-time, union, and non-resident aliens	Tax filing deadline, plus extensions	Yes, IRS form 5500 and other ERISA requirements	December 31st of the year you want to make contributions
401(k) Roth & Traditional	Employees can defer up to $18,000, catch-up contribution is $6,000 (50 or older). 25% of compensation (employee contributions are always 100% vested), may exceed $54,000	May be tax-deductible (pre-tax) or tax-free distribution (post-tax), vesting schedules allowed	Age 21 or older, worked 1 year with company. Can exclude part-time, union, and non-resident aliens	For employee deferrals it is each pay period, for sole proprietors when income is determined, employer contributions by tax deadline plus extensions	Yes, IRS form 5500 and other ERISA requirements	December 31st of the year you want to make contributions
Safe Harbor 401(k)	Employees can defer up to $18,000, catch-up contribution is $6,000 (50 or older). 25% of compensation and 20% for sole proprietors. Employer and employee to not exceed $54,000	May be tax-deductible (pre-tax) or tax-free distribution (post-tax), may allow for loans. Plan testing is not required.	Age 21 or older, worked 1 year with company. Can exclude part-time, union, and non-resident aliens	For employee deferrals it is each pay period, for sole proprietors when income is determined, employer contributions by tax deadline plus extensions	Yes, IRS form 5500 and other ERISA requirements	December 31st of the year you want to make the contributions

BONUS Material

As I get the opportunity to talk with many business owners I know they are busy and they often get so caught up in their work it is hard to see the big picture of what they need to do to protect what they've built. The business reflects who they are and the legacy they are leaving for their family.

Unfortunately, often what happens is a mess as they fail to do simple planning that would protect them against many of the mistakes I see. This section will cover many of those items and provide simple and inexpensive steps they can take to protect yourself.

My goal for business owners is to make sure they can compete in their current landscape. Have a system to protect their company against the unexpected and provide themselves with a comfortable retirement. There are certain things that all business owners should do to ensure continuation of their company.

This section will cover how to recruit top talent and reward them. You can use the ideas about non-qualified deferred compensation (NQDC) to supplement your retirement planning as well. In addition, risk measures to protect your company against the unexpected.

Talent hits a target no one else can hit; genius hits a target no one else can see- Arthur Schopenhauer

Read if:

- Over 50 employees or a group of highly compensated employees facing 401(k) contribution limits
- Typically, businesses at least 10 years old
- Looking to supplement your retirement plan

Rewarding Top Talent

When it comes to growing your business a key way to accomplish that is to bring top talent into your organization. While you might be a business of 2 or 3 employees currently you see a bigger company soon. This could be an organization of 10 or an organization of 1000 and to do that you must surround yourself with the best possible talent.

There are several reasons that you want to attract exceptional employees:

- Increased productivity and profitability
- Increased business valuation
- Replacement of key employees
- Incentivize key employees

What are the top talent looking for that you could deliver?

- Future retirement income
- Financial security for themselves and their family
- Future growth opportunities

Non-qualified Deferred Compensation/409(a) Plans

Non-qualified deferred compensation can get complicated so it is always a good idea to work with an advisor who is familiar with them. Since these are written plans, just like a 401(k), you will want to work with a knowledgeable TPA (third party administrator) who assures that the plan stays compliant.

In its simplest form a NQDC (non-qualified deferred compensation) plan can be any plan or arrangement that defers compensation and, with it, income tax to a later year. There are several NQDC plans to choose from including:

- Traditional non-equity unsecured and unfunded deferred compensation plans (voluntary salary, bonus plans, 401(k) mirror, supplemental defined benefit, excess benefit, stock phantom, etc...)
- Section 457(f) plans, these are top-hat plans maintained by not-for-profit and government plans
- Certain SAR's, these are stock appreciation rights issued at less than FMV (fair market value)
- Certain stock option plans, it depends on valuation of the stock and if there is deferral of income
- Some split dollar life insurance plans, take into consideration those that have an equity component
- Severance, if they don't fit within the exemptions parameters
- Miscellaneous deferral and supplemental arrangements in employment agreements
- Bonus, deferred stock, and miscellaneous other nonexempt compensation if it does not fall within the Short-Term Deferral exemption
- Reimbursements following separation from service, if the distributions are delayed beyond 2 years and more than 2x compensation

If all of that threw you for a loop you are not alone. That is why you work with someone to assist you with this process. The basics of a NQDC is that the company is making a legally binding contractual obligation to pay a future benefit, if an employee fulfills their end of the obligation. Rarely is there a formal funding process in order to avoid current taxation to the employee The employee is an unsecured creditor. The company often does an "informal" funding, this provides assurance to the employee that they will receive the benefit in the future. This is often done through a corporate owned life insurance (COLI) or a rabbi trust.

Why do companies choose permanent life insurance for these programs? There are benefits to permanent life insurance that people often shy away from because of the cost:

- Death benefit- provides an easy way to create a legacy for individuals and provides cash for companies looking to replace key employees.
- Investment account- permanent life insurance can have investment accounts that are invested in the market, track an index, or simply pay a set interest rate.
- Tax benefits- once the money is invested inside the account it is tax-deferred.
- Distributions- you can take a normal distribution or as a loan. This can be the difference between being taxed as normal income (beyond the cost basis) and tax-free. Talk to a professional about how it can help control your taxes in retirement.
    - These benefits apply to individuals, when held as deferred compensation the entire amount becomes taxable at distribution.

We'll review some of the more common NQDC plans and see how you could incorporate them into your business.

Bonus Deferral

A bonus deferral is an employer agreeing to pay an employee and an annual bonus (employee has the option to defer salary as well). Then at a point in the future, typically retirement, the employee is paid that bonus plus interest. When the money is paid out the employer can deduct the money paid and the employee must claim that as income.

Most of these plans are funded with life insurance. The business protects itself because if the key person passes away during their time with the company they get paid out the death benefit. The employee is happy because they get to supplement their retirement plan with additional compensation.

The company owns the life insurance policy and it is considered an asset of the company should they be targeted by creditors. Because the company owns the policy they don't receive an immediate tax deduction and the employee isn't taxed because they haven't received an actual benefit.

Employer Match

When they refer to a 401(k) mirror plan this is what they are referencing to. Just like with a 401(k) plan the TPA will draw up a plan outlining contribution amounts, match, vesting schedule, and distributions. The employee will defer a portion of their income or bonus, this amount will be match by the company. The company will then purchase a permanent life insurance to informally fund the policy. At the employee's retirement, the company can deduct the amount paid annually and the employee must report that amount as income.

SERP (Supplement Executive Retirement Plan)

For this plan, the employee does not have an option to contribute. The employer agrees to pay the employee additional benefits based on salary and years of service. The employee will receive those benefits upon retiring and dependent on the vesting schedule.

The policy can also be structured in such a way that it allows the company to recover its cost in the plan and still provide a benefit to the family.

Other Plans to consider

The executive bonus arrangement is the same concept in that you want to incentivize your employees. This plan avoids the administration of a 409(a), in exchange they also give-up control of the funding vehicle but they do receive an immediate tax-break instead of a deferred tax-break.

The company will reward a select group of key executives. The employer will make a tax-deductible contribution to pay the premium on a permanent life insurance policy. The employee pays income taxes on the amount paid, although employers do have the option to cover this amount. The life insurance policy is then held in the individual's name so they have immediate access to the funds. If they leave the policy funded and something happens to them, then the death benefits are paid directly to their beneficiaries.

You can also set these plans-up with the life insurance company so the funds are restricted from access by the employee. This provides a golden handcuff to keep employees with the company. Only after a certain number of years the key executives have access to the plan.

Split-dollar arrangement is a plan where the company purchases a permanent life insurance policy on the life of the executive and pays all the premiums. The company then endorses a portion to the executive as a pre-retirement survivor benefit. The executive is taxed on that amount either using rates based on a term policy or IRS table of rates. If the executive were to pass away the company receives part of the benefit that they can use as a key man policy. The executive's beneficiaries receive the balance. When the executive retires the arrangement is terminated. At that point in time the company can recover their cost through the death benefit or give the remainder of the policy to the executive as a taxable benefit.

Buy-Sell Strategies

Read if:

- *Everyone is required to read this, even if you are a sole proprietor*

A simple buy-sell strategy is often overlooked by business owners to protect their family should something happen. A buy-sell strategy is a life insurance policy purchased on the life of a business owner(s). The policy is owned by a key person, family member, or other business partners. These are important because:

- It guarantees a buyer upon an owner's death, retirement, or disability
- Creates liquidity for deceased owner's family
- Avoids valuation difficulties
- Solves lack of marketability issues

I see more issues where a business must be sold at a discount because business owners didn't take the simple steps to purchase a buy-sell agreement.

Part of the concern of a buy-sell is the cost of the life insurance. You have two options when it comes to life insurance. The first option is a term policy, these are policies designed for a certain number of years (10, 15, 20, 30 year). If you plan on being in business for a short time or you can't afford a permanent policy this is a good option. With the way that term policies are written today you can buy one that has a term-to-perm option. This means that you can convert the term policy into a permanent policy once the business is more established and you can afford the policy.

The second option is going with a permanent policy. This provides a couple of nice options. The first is that the death policy is there to protect the business owner's heirs. The other option is to use the cash value as collateral for a lifetime buyout of the company. Whatever way works for you and the budget of your company it is crucial to get a policy. It will work differently based on how many owners you have.

Keep in mind this is a brief overview. Dependent on how your business is set-up, how the insurance is funded, and other factors will affect the taxation of the policy. Please use this as a starting point to start a conversation with an expert in the field.

Sole Proprietor/One Way Buy-Sell

If you are the only owner of the company many people will wonder why they should worry about the buy-sell arrangement. It is important for single owner's because if they pass away there will be questions about:

- Difficulty in selling the business
- Paying any estate taxes
- Continuation or loss of the business

A buy-sell for an individual owner is established with a key employee or family member. That person would take a policy out on the business owner. The business bonuses the premium payments to the key employee or family member. Upon the business owner's death, they are required to purchase the business from the estate of the deceased owner and they are now the owner.

They may not want to own the business, but it does provide them a longer period to find a suitable buyer. If a family had to sell the business to pay estate taxes they typically have 9 months to complete the sale. With such a short time period, they aren't likely to get the true value of the company.

When the owner of a business passes away without a buy-sell it can strain the surviving family members. The salary from the owner suddenly stops, unless there is a solid succession plan in place. The business gets devalued because of the loss of a key employee. When money is the tightest there are still bills to pay for personal reasons and for the business. It can put a family in a real tough position. Even if the owner didn't have a family, this can put a strain on the executor of the estate.

Cross-Purchase Buy-Sell

An extremely simply concept. In this arrangement, the owners of the business buy insurance on each other and use death proceeds to purchase the deceased owners shares.

This works best when there are two to three owners.

I have seen multiple occasions where partnerships, LLC's, and S Corps were forced to liquidate their business because one business owner passed away. If you started a company and now it is worth $5 million, would you have the money to pay for your partners share and buy them out? If you already have a buy-sell is it up-to-date with the current value of your company? This is about making your family whole while allowing a business to survive and flourish.

Entity Redemption Buy-Sell Arrangement

Instead of individuals owning policies on each other. This arrangement has the business owning one policy on each owner. This works out better for companies with three or more owners. Once you get beyond three owners it becomes very expensive for the individual owners to purchase multiple policies. This provides a clean option for companies with multiple owners.

Cross Endorsed Buy-Sell Arrangement

Each owner owns their own life insurance policy, they end up "renting" a portion of the policy to the other business owners. The rented portion becomes a source of funds to purchase shares from the deceased owner. This is a tax neutral strategy when done properly.

Lifecycle Buy-Sell Strategy

This is a different policy from the typical buy-sell arrangement. All the other policies are either individually owned or owned by the company. With this policy, the owner creates a new business entity to own life insurance policies on each of their lives. The owners than contribute money each year to pay for the life insurance premiums. In the event of a buyout trigger, the cash value or death benefit can be used to fund the buyout.

The rationale behind this is that by having life insurance in a separate entity it protects the cash value in the life insurance from creditors. Also, if business owners are involved in multiple businesses together they can create a single point for life insurance. This will save on having multiple smaller valuation policies.

Key Takeaways

There isn't a superior policy, each one is designed for different businesses. The cost is surprisingly affordable and is much better option than the alternative of having to liquidate a business at fire sale prices. Remember estate taxes must be paid within 9 months of an owner's death often putting buyers in the driver's seat of determining the price they will pay.

It is important to get a business valuation every few years to make sure the buy-sell arrangement you originally signed-up for is valid. There are many insurance companies that will provide a complementary valuation. However, if the company becomes large it can be worth it to get a paid valuation. Please keep in mind that the complementary valuations are not IRS compliant and likely wouldn't hold-up in court.

Key Person

In several of the buy-sell strategies we mentioned key person. Who exactly is a key person? A key person is someone whose knowledge, work, or overall contribution is considered uniquely valuable to the company.

In many cases, this is the owner, but in some cases, it can be someone else. If you have a sales team of 8 people but 1 person is responsible for 70% of all sale that would be a key person. You can be confident that the company would suffer a significant set-back should that person unexpectedly die. You might also have someone who knows how to work their way around a complicated system. This could be electronic or simply bureaucratic, this unique skill set could be the reason a company continues to operate efficiently.

If you have someone on your team that does all of this, as a business owner, you want to make sure they are happy. In many cases you will be willing to give them a part of the business because you understand that their contributions are instrumental to the valuation of the company.

If that person was to die unexpectedly it would suffer a critical blow to the business and potentially take down the business depending on the size of its operations. That is where key man insurance comes into play.

Key man insurance is life insurance on a key person of the business. The money is designed to help the company cope with an unexpected loss and the monetary fall out that could result from this happening.

Key man insurance isn't about profiting off the loss of an employee passing away. This is about providing monetary inflow into the company until they can find a suitable replacement for the loss they just suffered. Many times, the replacement will come at a great cost and the life insurance money will help provide a float until the company gets back on solid footing.

A real-life example is a friend of mine started a company and worked tirelessly for three years to get it going. Just as things were clicking and the company started to take off he was killed in a car accident at the age of 35. At the time, he was married and had a young child, but he didn't have key man insurance. He never thought he would need it because of his age.

While in the middle of a tragic situation his wife had to pick-up the pieces to her personal life that had just been tragically torn apart. Then she was faced with the reality that she needed to run a business that she wasn't prepared to. With the help of friends and family they could keep the business afloat and make sure vendors and employees were paid.

It took a while for her to gain the expertise that she needed. It was a full two years before the business got back to the level it was at before he passed away.

Being young and healthy it would have been inexpensive for him to purchase a term policy until he could afford a permanent one. This would have helped the business initially instead of placing extra strain on the family when they were already suffering emotionally.

Like all insurance, it is designed to make you whole, not to profit from it. And my advice for anyone who is looking to get key man insurance is to get as much as you can. Start off with quotes from $100,000, $250,000, $500,000, and $1,000,000. You will be surprised at how affordable it can be and the level of comfort it provides knowing the company is looked after.

Other Important Coverages

Business Interruption Coverage

How long can you survive if outside forces interrupt your business operations. This can be anything from not having natural gas, phone outage, no water, or no electricity. Business interruption insurance can come into play with a natural disaster or just an isolated one. The coverage will look at historical financial statements to determine the amount paid. The key areas that it covers include:

- Profits that would have been earned
- Fixed costs-operating expenses
- Temporary location- if you must move to a temporary location
- Training cost associated with getting employees up-to-speed on new machinery installed after the disaster

This coverage is simply added to your existing property coverage. Talk to you agent to find out all the options available to you. Like a lot of insurance this can be customized to your specific situation.

Professional Liability Insurance

This is also known as errors & omissions (E&O) insurance. This will cover you for a failure to perform. This is insurance used in professional service offices. For example, if you visit an advisor and you find out later it cost thousands of dollars in unnecessary taxes because of the advice you received. E&O insurance would work to make the person whole, to the situation they were at before the poor advice.

This can also come into play if your company does a new marketing slogan and it happens to be like another company. If you are sued E&O insurance helps to cover those claims.

Even if you go to court over a claim of wrongdoing by a client and you are cleared, the cost for lawyers can be daunting. Especially if you are a young company trying to get your footing. The insurance would help to cover the cost of attorney.

Professional liability insurance comes in many shapes and sizes so make sure to talk to your agent about your specific company and how it can play a key role in helping your situation.

Product Liability Insurance

If you are manufacturing anything than this is an important coverage to have. Even if you take every precaution, more than likely there will be a lawsuit at some point in the products life. This makes sure that you are covered if found liable for any damage because of producing your product.

Home-based businesses

It is fun to read about great businesses that started in a house or in a garage. This is the case for Google, Apple, Amazon, Disney, Yankee Candle and many more. Whether you are a start-up tech company or a start-up candle company you need to make sure the business that you have started so far will survive and thrive.

Your homeowner's insurance doesn't cover home-based businesses. You will want to make sure you talk to your agent about adding insurance to cover your small business. Otherwise the equipment and inventory that you have invested in will not be covered in the event of a problem.

Success usually comes to those who are too busy to be looking for it-Henry David Thoreau

Final Thoughts

You are small business and you are a big deal. You owe it to yourself to make sure you have the correct financial framework to succeed. You have a passion to go out and make your own mark on the world. Make sure you make that mark, change the world from the way we currently see it.

The beautiful thing about this nation is that we can go from nothing to something. If you have shared your vision with a 100-other people and they said you can't do it, guess what, it doesn't matter. This quest that you are on is between you and you. You can move mountains, you can accomplish whatever you set your mind to.

I feel privileged to work with business owners. The opportunity to see the growth that they experience from year-to-year. To see the struggle and eventually the glory. I can't put in the long hours for the business owner, but I can make sure they have the framework in place to be successful.

About the Author

Matthew Meyers is a business owner who has started, and sold, various businesses during his lifetime. His true passion has always been about helping others. He can fulfill that passion through personal finance. He has counseled thousands of individuals and couples in their pursuit of better financial management.

With a degree in business from Western Michigan University, an MBA, and his certification as a Certified Financial Planner™ Matthew uses his education and experience to coach his clients. An avid reader, he stays on top of trends (good and bad) that influence the behavior of his clients.

With a thriving practice and constant development of new products to assist his clients, Matthew looks forward to everyday and the difference he can make